Literature-Based Theme Unit

The Alien Logs of Super Jewels

Book by BK Bradshaw
Educational Materials by Rebecca Detwiler
& Dr. Brenda Bradshaw

INFINITY KIDS PRESS

Literature-Based Theme Unit: The Alien Logs of Super Jewels

Copyright © Rebecca Detwiler & Dr. Brenda Bradshaw, 2020

ISBN 13: 978-0-9994098-3-1

PUBLISHER'S NOTE: Without limiting the rights under the copyright reserved above, no part of this publication may be reproduced, stored in or introduced into a retrieval system, or transmitted, in any form or by any means (electronic, mechanical, photocopying, recording or otherwise), without the prior written permission of both the copyright owner and the above publisher of this book.

Infinity Kids Press
www.bkbradshaw.com
www.super-jewels.com

Printed in the United States of America

Table of Contents

Introduction – Book Synopsis, Objectives, Vocabulary, Resources, About Autism	1
Alien Log #1: Alien Vs. Superhero – Character Study	3
Alien Log #2: Art, Darts & Cat's Paws – Making Comparisons	4
Alien Log #3: Kinderprison – Flashbacks, Character Feelings & Traits	5
Alien Log #4: How Can I Sleep When I'm Thinking About Unicorn Pegasuses – Finding Evidence	7
Alien Log #5: My Favorite Color Is Rainbow - Comparing with Similes	8
Alien Log #6: Breaking News - Personification	9
Alien Log #7: The Fish Lady Plays Like Fireworks – Nicknames, Unexpected Reactions & Creative Response	10
Alien Log #8: My Brain Might Be a Cheeseburger – Whimsical Words	13
Alien Log #9: Autism Is Not Aweseometism - Comparing & Contrasting	14
Alien Log #10: Not-So-Super Jewels – What's Your Superpower? & Coping with Change	15
Alien Log #11: Cupcake – Fluffy Friends, Character Traits, 4-line Poem	17
Alien Log #12: Fast-Forward to Fourth Grade – Making Friends	19
Alien Log #13: Besties – Making Friends, Similes & Metaphors	20
Alien Log #14: I Hate My Mother's S's – Managing Emotions, Stating and Supporting Your Opinions	21
Alien Log #15: Camp Inspire – Trying Something New	22
Alien Log #16: Social Skills Are Definitely Not My Superpower – Did I Say That Out Loud?	23
Alien Log #17: Muddle School – Coping with Change	24
Alien Log #18: Champion Vs. Villain – Making Friends	25
Alien Log #19: Being Flexible Is Definitely Not My Superpower – Making Friends	26
Alien Log #20: Infinity Meltdowns – Descriptive Words	27
Alien Log #21: Homeschooling – Coping with Change	28
Alien Log #22: Drum Roll, Please – Accepting Yourself, Supporting Details	29
Afterthoughts: Main Theme, Using Text Evidence	31
Word Search	32
Acrostic	33
A-MAZE-ING Avengers (Maze)	34

Copyright 2020 Infinity Kids Press

Introduction

Book Synopsis

Why does everything seem so easy for everyone else? As Jewels recounts her adventures from Kinderprison to Muddle School, she looks for clues to what sets her apart. Could she be an alien, a superhero, or something completely different?

Join Jewels as she explores the confusing—and often hilarious—world of social expectations. Jewels' journey of self-discovery takes her to some unexpected places, and most surprising of all is finding a little bit of ourselves along the way.

Objectives for Reading *The Alien Logs of Super Jewels*

1. Introduce Autism/Asperger's Syndrome and the underlying reasons for the behaviors of those with autism.
2. Reduce bullying behaviors through knowledge and understanding.
3. Increase acceptance of diverse populations.

Vocabulary to Think About Before Reading the Book to Children

Autism/Asperger's syndrome – According to the Autistic Self-Advocacy Network (ASAN), autism is a neurological variation that occurs in approximately 1% of the population and is classified as a developmental disability. **Asperger's syndrome** (AS) was a subclass of autism prior to 2013, when it was removed from the Diagnostic & Statistical Manual of Mental Disorders (DSM) and simply included under the umbrella term, "autism spectrum disorder." Many individuals who were originally diagnosed using the term, "Asperger's," still identify with the term. Some shorten the term to "Aspie." (See page 2 for a more detailed explanation of the characteristics of autism.

bullying – To use superior strength or influence to intimidate (someone), typically to force him or her to do what one wants.

diversity – The state of having a variety or range of different things.

Resources for Research Prior to Teaching

Autistic Self-advocacy Network (ASAN) - https://autisticadvocacy.org/

Neurotribes: The Legacy of Autism and the Future of Neurodiversity, by Steve Silberman - https://www.stevesilberman.com/books/#neurotribes

Loud Hands: Autistic People Speaking - https://autisticadvocacy.org/book/loud-hands-autistic-people-speaking/

Introduction

Thank you for your interest in teaching children about the diverse populations of our world and increasing their understanding, respect, and admiration of those who may be different from the norm.

More than 1% (1 in 58) of the world population has the neurodivergent characteristics of someone autistic. It occurs at the same rate across all races and socioeconomic income levels.

Children with autism have the same range of intellectual abilities as the general population. They may have low intellectual ability, be gifted, or anywhere in between. Most individuals with autism can still fully participate in school, work, hobbies, and relationships.

These typical characteristics of an individual with autism occur in varying degrees in each person:

- **Sensory perception and integration differences** – They may have heightened sensitivity or also be sensory seeking. For example, they may love loud noises, or avoid loud noises, or vacillate between the two.
- **Narrow, intense interests** – They may be able to focus intensely on an area of interest for prolonged periods of time and show little interest in anything else. For example, whereas a typical child might practice the piano for 15-30 minutes, a child on the autism spectrum might play for hours. This can be a obvious strength for talent development.
- **Asynchronous development** – They may have giftedness in one or more areas, but demonstrate disability in others. For example, they may be able to calculate large numbers quickly, but have difficulty with handwriting because of poor fine motor function. Because this is how they are "wired," it is best to focus on strength-based learning rather than spending long hours trying to remediate deficits.
- **Atypical social behaviors and interactions** – They may prefer to be alone most of the time and function better in quieter, less social environments. They may find social interaction exhausting due to their difficulty with interpreting elements of social communication such as nonverbal clues (facial expressions, posture, etc.) and non-literal oral communication (idioms, slang, sarcasm, etc.). They may have difficulty waiting their turn, participating in small talk, and adhering to social conventions if they do not seem logical and/or meaningful. Teaching typical kids about autistic communication tends to be more beneficial in improving social interactions than spending long hours teaching those with autism social skills.
- **Repetitive movements** – They may "stim," or flap their hands, twiddle their fingers, rock, or spin. This is to be encouraged because it helps them regulate themselves.
- **Need for routines and predictability** – They may prefer to have things happen in the same order and in the same manner each time they occur. For example, they may need their morning routine to be exactly the same every day or they become intensely anxious. This also means they can be very dependable and reliable in keeping with routines.
- **Divergent thinking** – "Thinking outside the box" comes easily for autistic individuals. Possibly because they are not overly concerned with social impact, children with autism tend to think and express themselves freely, resulting in remarkably uninhibited creative work and problem solving. Their typical ability to attend to detail can also be an asset in projects or activities calling for these skills.

Children with autism are loving, caring individuals who have the same needs and desires of all other children. They are active contributors to our society and are welcome members of our classroom communities!

Alien Log #1: Alien Vs. Superhero

Character Study

This story is told from 1st person point of view.

1. From what you have read so far, who is the narrator and what are two things you know about her?

Vocabulary Focus

extraterrestrial
Asperger's syndrome
abilities
evidence

2. List two words that describe Jewels' tone or personality?

3. Why is Jewels writing her Alien Log?

4. Since this story is told from Jewels' perspective, how will this make the story unique? Will we always be able to believe her?

Your Alien Log:
What would you like to understand better about yourself? Start your own Alien Log here!

Alien Log #2:
Art, Darts & Cat's Paws

Making Comparisons

Jewels is not a typical child. Complete the comparison chart of an average toddler and Jewels. In this chapter, what did we learn about her artistic ability, throwing aim and things that she was interested in as a young child?

Vocabulary Focus

city skyline
jabber box
abducted

Typical Kid	Jewels

Your Alien Log:

Ask your parent/guardian what you were like as a child, and create your log here!

Alien Log #3: Kinderprison

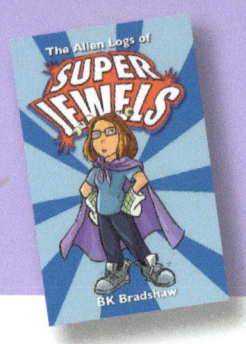

Flashbacks

This chapter begins with a flashback, or goes back in time to tell the story. What is the setting of this log?

Time:

Place:

Vocabulary Focus
- fluttered
- dangled
- mobiles
- occupied
- crouching

Character Feelings

How does Jewels feel in Kindergarten? Describe her experiences in school and use text evidence to support your answer. Example: Jewels felt annoyed because she was forced to take a nap even though she wasn't tired.

Jewels feels...	Page #	Evidence

Your Alien Log:

How do you feel at school? List evidence to support your answer.

Alien Log #3: Kinderprison

Character Traits

We learn about a main character based on what the character **thinks** or **says**, things the character **does**, and what **other characters say** about the character. In this book, Jewels is convinced she is either an alien from another planet or a superhero. Complete the web with examples of Jewels' unique abilities and characteristics that make her feel different from other kids. (Example: amazing artist)

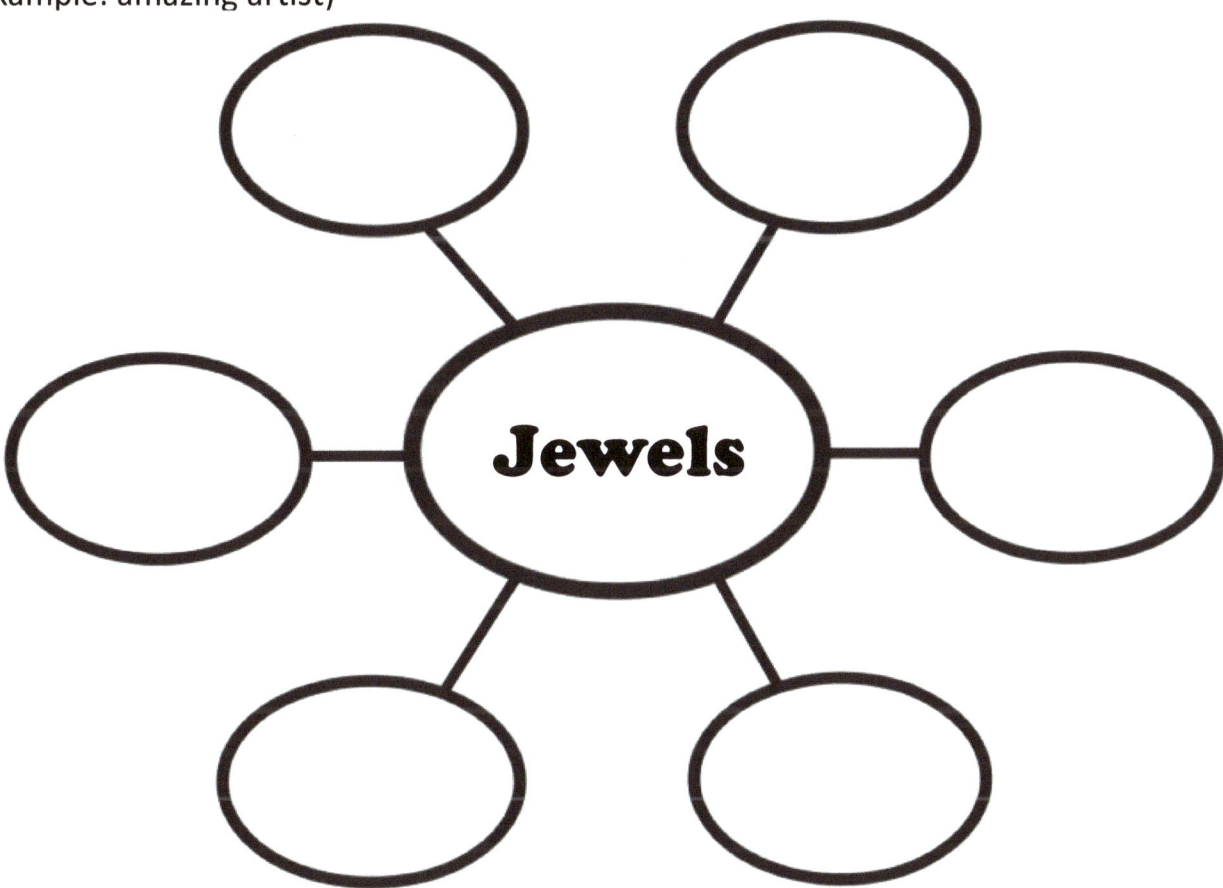

Your Alien Log:
What are some of your special abilities or interests?

Alien Log #4:
How Can I Sleep When I'm Thinking About Unicorn Pegasuses?

Finding Evidence

Why can't Jewels sleep in this chapter?

Based on her actions and what she says, how would you describe Jewels' imagination?

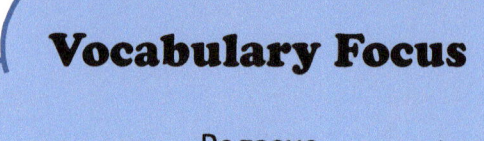

Vocabulary Focus

Pegasus

Find a quote from this chapter to back up your opinion.

Page #	Quote	This shows...

Your Alien Log:
Have you ever been unable to sleep? If so, why?

Alien Log #5:
My Favorite Color Is Rainbow

Comparing with Similes

Similes compare two things using the words "like" or "as."

Find similes in this chapter and log them below. Two examples are provided. Feel free to make up your own.

Vocabulary Focus

lavender
glitch

Similes
"Purple was happy like a rainbow."
"Fold the paper like a hamburger."

Your Alien Log:

What is your favorite color? _____ Write a simile to show why you like the color.
Example: Yellow is warm like the sun.

Alien Log #6: Breaking News

Personification

Personification is when you attribute human characteristics to non-human objects.

Why does Jewels say, "Breaking News—I'm a pig."?

Vocabulary Focus

mimicked
villain
appropriate
quirkiest

On page 41, Jewels says, "I put the dress on and it attacked me!"

Use details from the text to explain why Jewels felt the dress "attacked" her.

Page	Text Support

Your Alien Log:

What is one of your favorite things, like a keepsake or item in your room? Describe it using personification. *Example: My favorite video game was hiding under my books.*

Alien Log #7:
The Fish Lady Plays Like Fireworks

Nicknames

Jewels often gives people nicknames using words that she thinks about when she hears their names. Explain why Jewels gave these characters their nicknames:

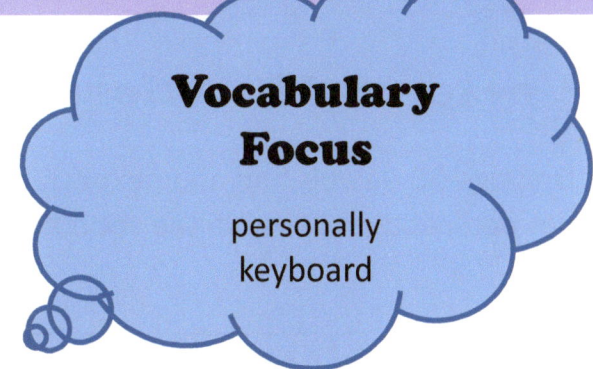

Vocabulary Focus

personally
keyboard

Name	Why does Jewels call the person this?
Hannah "Banana" Akers	
Michael "Spider" Webb	
Gretchen "Perfect" Shelton	
"Fish Lady"	

How do you think the other characters feel about the nicknames Jewels has given them?

Your Alien Log:

Do you have a nickname? How did you get the nickname? Do you like being called that name? Why or why not?

Alien Log #7:
The Fish Lady Plays Like Fireworks

Unexpected Reactions

On page 50, Jewels had an unexpected reaction to the piano music. From her perspective, describe the sounds and describe her reactions.

Sounds	Jewels' Reactions

Why do you think Jewels had these reactions?

Why do you think Jewels says, "Sometimes I think music is the language of my home planet."?

Your Alien Log:

Have you ever had an unexpected reaction to something? Describe your reaction. Why do you think you reacted that way?

Alien Log #7:
The Fish Lady Plays Like Fireworks

Creative Response – Shooting Stars

The last four verses of Jewels' song say:

> *Everyone is special*
> *For who they are*
> *And that's what makes them*
> *Shooting stars!*

Write a classmate's name on the star below. Think of positive characteristics about the student and write them on the tail of the star.

Alien Log #8:
My Brain Might Be a Cheeseburger

Whimsical Words

Jewels creates a whimsical tone on page 64 when she says, "Autism is awesometism!"

autism + awesome = awesometism

Create some whimsically combined words of your own. Think of an adjective and combine it with the ending of a noun.

Vocabulary Focus

patient
comfy
therapists
criteria

Adjective	Noun	New Word
wonderful	summer	wondesummerful

Your Alien Log:

Jewels always likes her ice cream the same way—"Mint chocolate chip in a regular cone." Is there anything you always like the same way?

Alien Log #9:
Autism Is Not Awesometism

Comparing and Contrasting

Comparing is showing how things are **alike**. Contrasting is showing how things are **different**.

On pages 69-71, Jewels experiences two different settings—Disneyland and her hotel room. Compare and contrast these two places according to how Jewels experiences them through her five senses.

Vocabulary Focus

unbelievably
bazillion
souvenirs

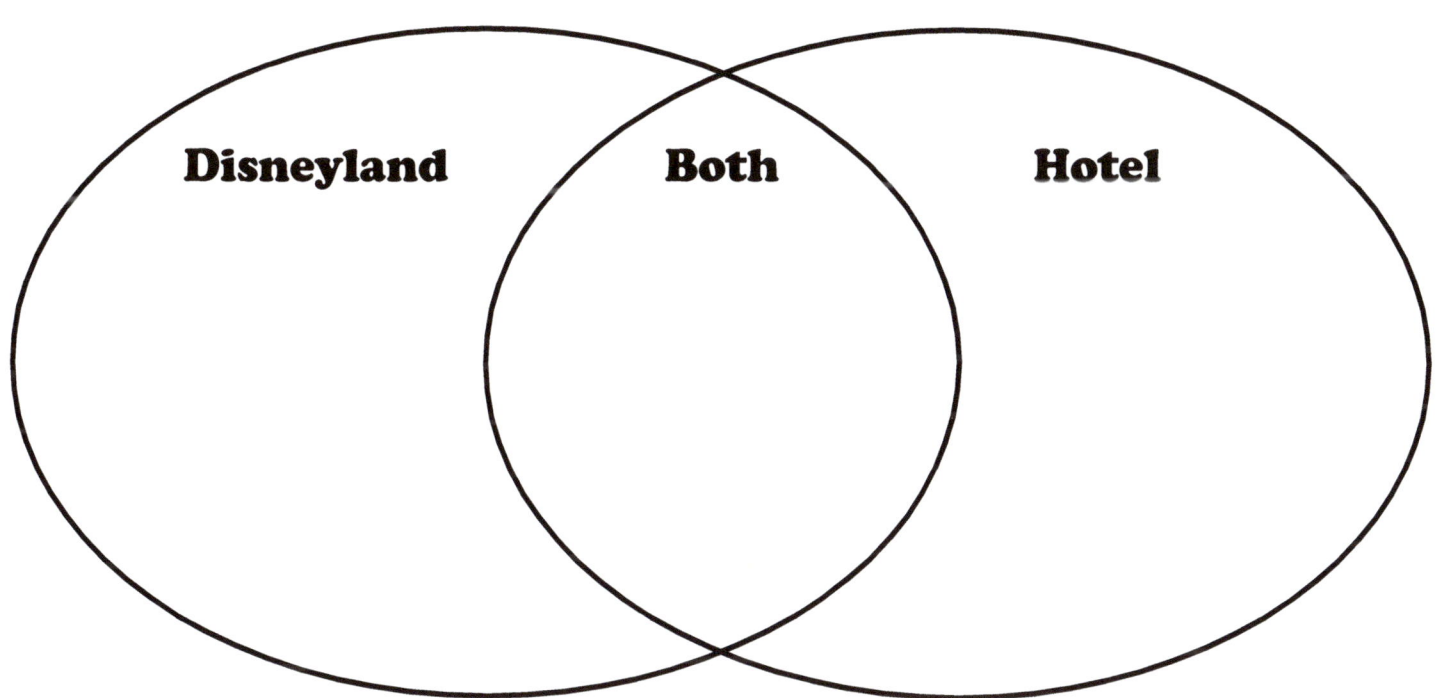

Your Alien Log:
Describe how you feel before, during and after going to a crowded public place like a mall, theme park, or busy restaurant.

Before:

During:

After:

14
Copyright 2020 Infinity Kids Press

Alien Log #10:
Not-So-Super Jewels

What's Your Superpower?

In this log, Jewels makes a list of her "autism superpowers." What is something you are good at? How does it help you at school, with family, or with friends? Write about it in the bubble below.

Vocabulary Focus

mimicking
defeat
invisible
dreadlocks
permission

Your Alien Log:
What superpower would you like to have and why?

Alien Log #10:
Not-So-Super Jewels

Coping with Change

In the 3rd grade, there are many changes to Jewels' school routines because of new teachers. Explain the changes caused by each teacher and how Jewels feels about these changes.

Vocabulary Focus
- mimicking
- defeat
- invisible
- dreadlocks
- permission

Character	Changes	Jewels feels...
Michael Spider Webb		
Mrs. Stone		
Ms. Rita		
Mrs. Dominguez		

Your Alien Log:
Are you flexible? How do you feel about changes?

Alien Log #11: Cupcake

Fluffy Friends

Who is Cupcake?

Name four things Jewels loved about Cupcake and describe how each attribute helped her.

Vocabulary Focus
- allergic
- hypoallergenic
- hybrid
- kryptonite

Characteristic of Cupcake	How It Helps Jewels

Which characteristic of Cupcake is most important?

Create an award for Cupcake and explain why she deserves it.

Certificate

Alien Log #11:
Cupcake

4-line Poem

Who is someone who supports and helps you?

Brainstorm 3 ways that this person helps you and write a 4-line poem that thanks them. For example:

You never tell my secrets
You like me even when I'm mad
You shower me with kindness
You're the best sister I could ever have

Your Alien Log:
Do you have a pet? If not, if you could have a pet, what pet would you like to have? Describe how your pet looks and behaves, or would look or behave if you had one.

Alien Log #12: Fast-Forward to Fourth Grade

Making Friends

Jewels always calls Gretchen, "Gretchen Perfect Shelton."
Does Gretchen think she is perfect? Why or why not?

Vocabulary Focus

pothole
allowance
series
illustrations

Name 3 things Gretchen and Jewels have in common:

1.

2.

3.

What does Jewels learn about Michael?

How does this change the way she views him?

Your Alien Log:
Have you ever changed your feelings and view about someone? Describe the person before and after you changed. What made you change?

Alien Log #13: Besties

More about Making Friends

Jewels and Gretchen become great friends in this chapter. Describe some of the things they do together.

Vocabulary Focus
trampoline
tingling
avenger

What secret does Gretchen know about Jewels and why is this important?

Similes and Metaphors

We learned that similes describe things using the words "like" or "as." Metaphors describe things without using the words "like" or "as."
For example:

      simile – Friendship is *like* a map that guides you through life.
      metaphor – Friendship is a map that guides you through life.

Write a simile and a metaphor about friendship:

Simile –

Metaphor –

Your Alien Log:

Have you ever trusted a friend with a secret? Did they keep it? Without revealing your secret, explain how you feel about sharing secrets.

Alien Log #14:
I Hate My Mother's S's

Managing Emotions

Jewels is angry in this chapter. What is one thing that is really REALLY driving her nuts?

Vocabulary Focus

hissing
desensitize
Inappropriate
elixir

How does Jewels learn to desensitize herself to sounds that bother her?

Stating and Supporting Your Opinions

On page 109, Dr. Silver says that having autism wasn't an excuse to do inappropriate things. Do you agree or disagree with this statement? Write an opinion statement and back it up with a support detail.

I think…

The reason I think this is because…

Your Alien Log:
What is one thing that bothers or distracts you and how do you cope with it?

Alien Log #15: Camp Inspire

Trying Something New

List four fun things that Jewels got to do at camp.

1.

2.

3.

4.

Give an example of how Jewels challenged herself to go outside of her comfort zone.

On page 123, what did Jewels discover that made her feel not so alone?

What are some reasons people often don't want to try something new?

What do you feel is the most important reason to try something new?

Vocabulary Focus
karaoke
recommended
sing-songy
zip-lining
brochure
pterodactyl
s'mores

Your Alien Log:
Describe the first time you tried something that became one of your favorite things.

Alien Log #16:
Social Skills Are Definitely Not My Superpower

Did I Say That Out Loud?

Vocabulary Focus

compliment

In this chapter, Jewels makes some rules to help her work on social skills. Think of a situation where someone says something that should have been thought and not voiced. Draw a 3-panel comic depicting the situation and use talk bubbles to show the right Vs. wrong responses.

Example: You see an older person struggling to carry their groceries.
Wrong response – "Wow! You're old!"
Right response – "May I help you with your groceries?"

Your Alien Log:

Have you ever said anything you wished you hadn't? If not, can you imagine how it would feel? Explain your answer.

Alien Log #17: Muddle School

Coping with Change, Take 2

Why does Jewels refer to middle school as "muddle school"?

List five things about elementary school that Jewels liked and how they changed in middle school.

Vocabulary Focus
- automatic
- detention
- disorganized
- muddled
- stairwell
- invisibility

Elementary School	Middle School

Your Alien Log:

Name a big change you have been through (like changing classrooms or schools, moving to a new house, etc.) and describe how you felt about the change. What did you do to cope with the change?

Alien Log #18: Champion Vs. Villain

Making Friends, Take 2

In what ways is Jewels like a villain to Michael?

Vocabulary Focus
nibbled
anxiety
miserable
millisecond

How could Jewels become a champion for Michael?

In the bubbles below, list five characteristics of superheroes that Jewels has.

Your Alien Log:
Think of someone in your life who could use a champion. Name one thing your could do to be a champion for that person.

Alien Log #19:
Being Flexible Is Definitely Not My Superpower

Making Friends, Take 3

What are three things that bother Jewels about physical education?

1.

2.

3.

On page 148, what advice does Jewels' mom give her?

What surprising thing does Jewels discover about dodgeball?

At the end of this chapter, what did Jewels do that finally made Michael smile?

Vocabulary Focus

physical education
nakedness
required
gymnasium

Your Alien Log:

Is there something you would like to do but it would make you nervous, anxious, or scared? What could you do to overcome it?

Alien Log #20: Infinity Meltdowns

Descriptive Words

List as many words as you can think of that could describe a "meltdown."

Vocabulary Focus

panic
trance
portal

What triggered the meltdown at the beginning of the chapter?

When she visited her old school, how did Jewels feel about her old "prison" now that she was in middle school? Give examples to support your answer.

What does Jewels mean when she says, "If the fourth stall was my 'portal potty,' it was closed forever."?

Your Alien Log:
What do you do to prevent yourself from having a meltdown?

Alien Log #21: Homeschooling

Coping with Change

Why do you think Jewels' parents pulled her out of school?

Vocabulary Focus
stress
existed
infinity
lactose intolerant

Name three things Jewels liked about homeschooling:

1.

2.

3.

On page 161, why did Jewels feel lucky for the first time ever?

How was homeschooling like an "epic parallel universe"?

Your Alien Log:
What are some reasons you feel lucky?

Alien Log #22:
Drum Roll, Please

Accepting Yourself

In this chapter Jewels compares autism to a rainbow. How is autism like a rainbow?

What does Jewels learn about Gretchen and Michael?

How does this make her feel about autism?

When Jewels went back to school, list five things that she had never noticed before.

1.

2.

3.

4.

5.

Why do you think she suddenly noticed these things?

Vocabulary Focus
IEP
spectrum
universe
peer mediator
enhanced
conquer
injustice

Your Alien Log:
What are some reasons you feel lucky?

Alien Log #22: Drum Roll, Please

Supporting Details

On page 168, Raphi compares Jewels to a superhero and gives her a purple cape. Name four of the superhero character traits that he sees in her and support details to back it up. The first one is done for you.

Superhero Trait	Support Detail
Enhanced senses	You are picky about tastes and smells and tags in your shirts and elastic and loud lockers.

On page 170, Jewels discovers her secret weapon. What is it?

How did Jewels' opinion of herself change from the beginning of the book to the end of the book?

    In the beginning she thought...

    In the end she thought...

Your Alien Log:
Do you have any of the superhero traits Raphi listed? Explain your answer.

Afterthoughts...

What do you think is the main theme (lesson) of this novel? Write a 3-paragraph essay that explains a theme from the book. Find specific text evidence and at least one quote from the novel to support your theme. Use the space below to plan, and write your essay on a separate paper.

Theme	
Text Evidence	
Text Evidence	
Quote	
Conclusion	

Word Search

EXTRATERRESTRIAL
ASPERGERS
MUDDLE
PURPLE
ALIEN
SUPERHERO
GLITCH
RAINBOW

CHAMPION
VILLAIN
UNICORN
JEWELS
MICHAEL
HANNAH
GRETCHN
RAPHI

STARDUST
BRAIN
AWESOMETISM
DISNEYLAND
INFINITY
INVISIBLE
FLEXIBLE
CUPCAKE

AVENGER
SENSITIVE
CAMP INSPIRE
S'MORES
SOCIAL SKILLS
MELTDOWN
CAPE
PORTAL

ANXIETY
UNIVERSE
GALAXY
SPECTRUM
PICKY
PERFECT
CAMP
EPIC

```
L C U P C A K E S R E V I N U L U H R L
F V W R L U L O D K V V F O A J P T A L
D Z Z W F P C H T D I V O I J Z K K C J
Q C K E R I P S N I T Y R P U O R F E H
R L S U A T U K M S I T E M O S E W A J
S D P L S D F A A N S I H A C I E H N B
L Z E G R E T C H E N N R H N L L U R R
A F C A M P J H R Y E I E C S X B A G K
T Q T R D M W R P L S F P V S K I L L S
R S R E G R E P S A B N U L I N X E I A
O H U H W T O L I N V I S I B L E B T D
P O M N A V H M T D I O N O I L L D C Y
E Q A R I N I I B D M G W F D V F A H Q
R O T I M C N X G H O U H D Y Z P V I N
F X Y S H P O A F N R W U D E E G E I N
E K Y A R N L R H Y E M N N P P X N I R
C N E I L A J Z N G S L M K Y Y O G R R
T L D F X E P I C K Y I E M P F X E T A
O A X Y B E I H O N T X H E L F P R F X
J S I I W B Y W I I P O H O V O V W M A
```

Acrostic

An acrostic is a poem or story that is written so that the first words in each line spell out a word or phrase. For example:

Brave is how I feel when I
Reach up to the stars
And set goals for myself, even if I am
Very afraid of failure, I am
Eager to complete the quest.

Now it is your turn! Select an word from the story and create an acrostic to demonstrate understanding of the word.

A-MAZE-ING AVENGERS

Help Jewels find the way to her favorite avengers—her family!

www.ingramcontent.com/pod-product-compliance
Lightning Source LLC
Chambersburg PA
CBHW041436010526
44118CB00002B/89